Magic Reader

Smart Alec

written by Danny Katz
illustrated by Mitch Vane

Desk Copy Request / Information

To place your desk copy request or for more information,
please contact the following office:
Tel : (02)3273-4300   Fax : (02)3273-4303

Contents

Welcome to Magic Reader

Character sketches provide prior information about the main characters

Repetitive and straightforward story lines

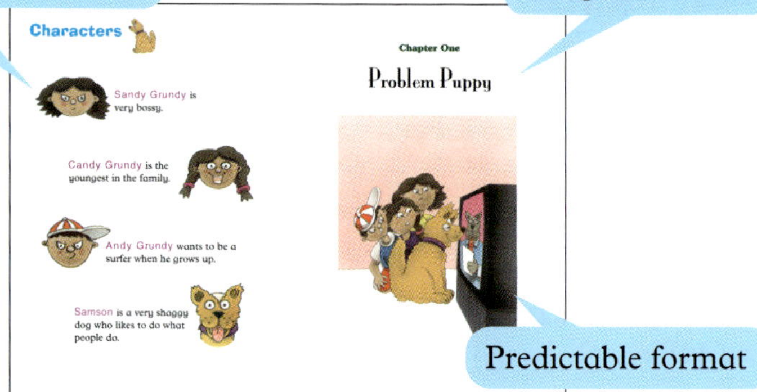

Predictable format

Familiar content related to everyday experiences

Full-color illustrations

Simply constructed sentences

A variety of simple sentence patterns

Includes oral and written language patterns

Use of high-frequency words

How to Use Magic Reader

Step 1. Listen to the Story

You'll love listening to the audio as you follow the flow of the story, even if you don't understand every single word or sentence.

Step 2. Read along with the Story

While improving your pronunciation and your ability to memorize sentences, you'll build confidence as you listen to and then read along with the audio in a loud voice.

Step 3. Listen to Specific Parts of Each Chapter

With each chapter broken up into sections, you'll be able to fully understand the meaning of each part as you listen.

Step 4. Try the Activity Questions

Make sure you fully understand the meaning of each story by doing the accompanying exercises.

Characters 

Smart Alec
knows everything
about everything.

Her **little brothers** would
like to get the better of
Smart Alec.

Barney Gavarney
is Smart Alec's good friend.

Chapter One

The Smartest Kid

MR-G1-01-1
MP3

Alec was smart. She was the
smartest kid in all the land.

She knew everything
about everything.

Her little brothers were playing
in the living room with their
spacemen.

Smart Alec stomped into the room
and said to them, "I bet you don't
know what the moon is made of."

"Well," Smart Alec said, "the moon is a giant banana. That's the truth. And lots of monkeys live on the moon and they lick the banana."

"That's why the moon is so shiny.
It's sparkling clean from all that
licking. So there! I bet you didn't
know that."

Smart Alec stomped out.

There was something she didn't know.

Her little brother had tied a thread

from her dress to the chair leg.

Chapter Two

The Loose Thread

MR-G1-01-1
MP3

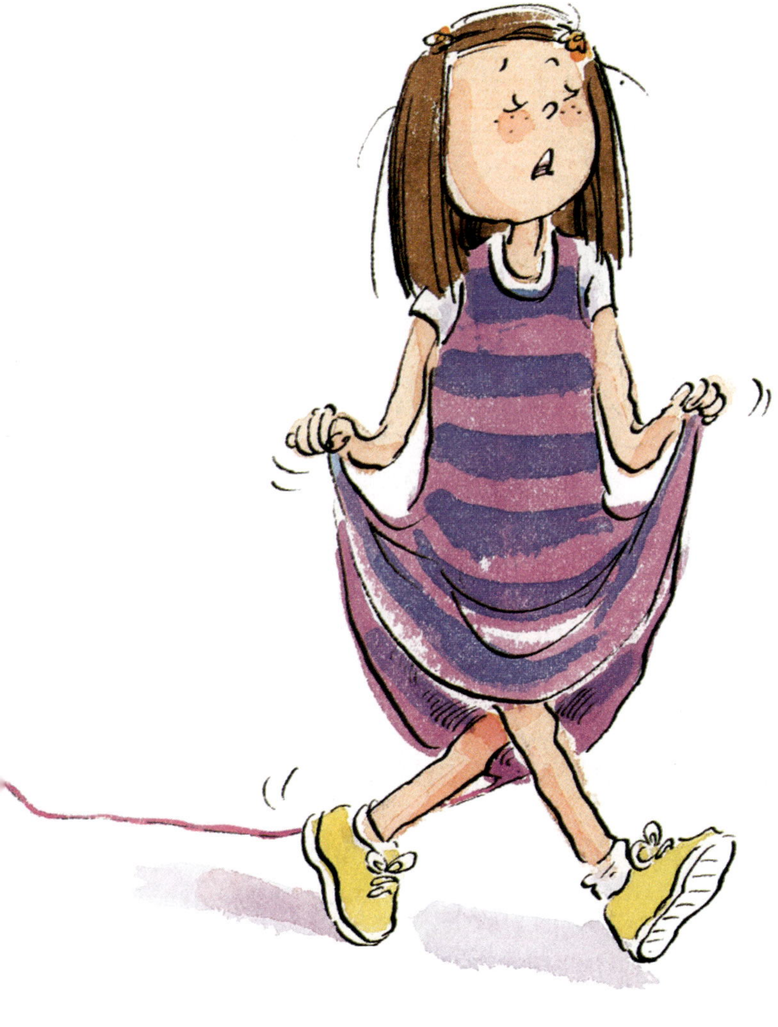

Alec's big sister was sitting in the
kitchen. She was eating toast for
breakfast.

Smart Alec strutted in and said,
"I bet you don't know what
happens if you eat too much toast.
Well, I know."

"You get a terrible stomachache.
Then suddenly all the toast pops out
of your belly button. So there!"

Smart Alec picked up her lunch
box and headed for the door.

She didn't know that the thread
from her dress was getting
longer and longer. It tangled itself
around pieces of furniture.

Chapter Three

Off to School

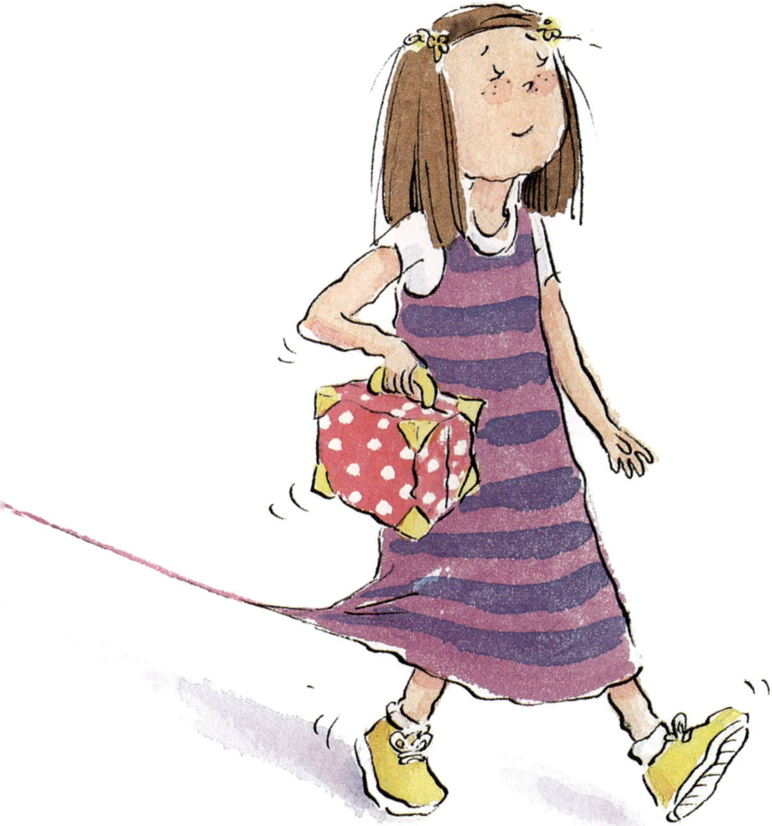

When Alec got to school,
her friend Barney Gavarney
was weeding the flower boxes.

Smart Alec stopped right by him
and said, "I bet you don't know
what flowers do at night.
Well, I know what flowers do at night."

"As soon as everyone's gone to bed,
all the flowers climb out of the ground.
They play games and have races.
That's the truth."

"Then the flowers go back into the ground before anyone wakes up. That's why they've got dew on them. They're so sweaty from all that running around. So there!"

Smart Alec kept walking. She didn't
know that the thread from her dress
had wound its way through the
school gate and round a tree.

Chapter Four

Chasing Butterflies

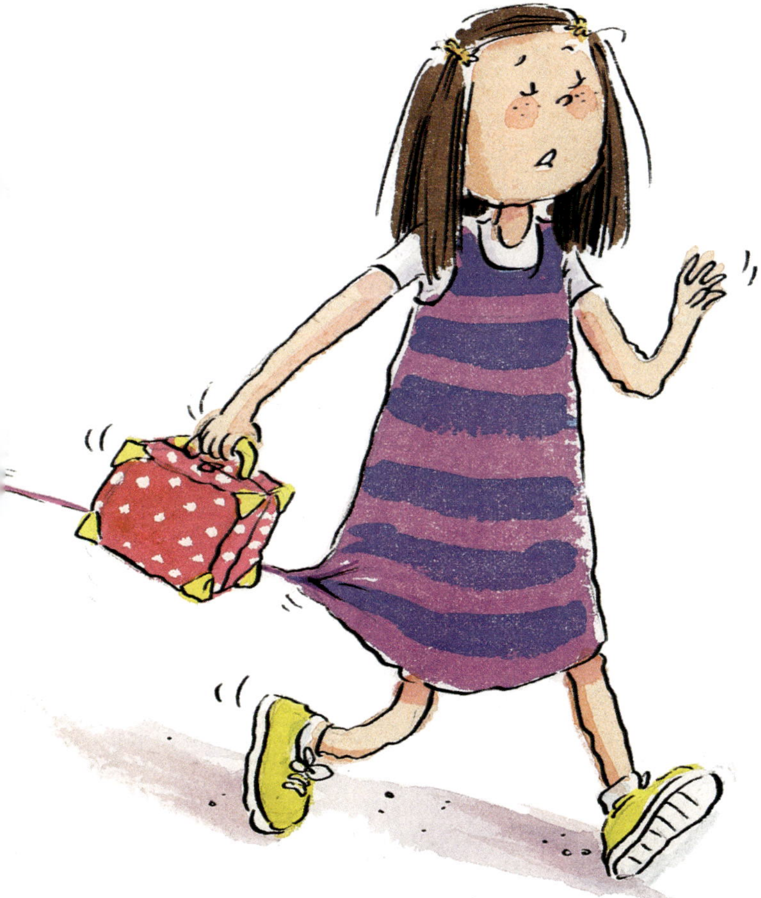

A dog ran onto the playground.
It was happily chasing butterflies
through the bushes.

Smart Alec marched over to the dog.
She said, "I bet you don't know how
to catch a butterfly."

"Well, I know how to
catch a butterfly. I'll show you."
She chased the butterflies.

She chased them round and round
and round the bushes.

Round and round and round
and round, she went.

She didn't know that the thread from
her dress was unwinding as she ran.
Soon there was hardly any dress left.

Not so smart, Alec.

EXERCISES

Name ___________________

What happened next?

Number the statements in their correct order so that they retell the story from Smart Alec.

The thread from her dress had wound its way through the school gate and around a tree.

Smart Alec told Barney Gavarney how the flowers ran around at night.

Smart Alec still did not know that a thread from her dress was unwinding, until there was hardly any dress left. Not so smart, Alec.

Smart Alec's dress got tangled around the furniture.

She told a tall tale about why the moon is so shiny.

Her little brother tied a thread from her dress to the chair leg.

Smart Alec thinks that she knows everything.

Smart Alec even showed a dog how to chase butterflies.

What is she like?

How do we find out about the character of Smart Alec?

What the pictures tell us

What the story tells us

I can't believe it!

Danny Katz (the author of Smart Alec*) uses exclamation marks in the story to highlight something that Alec is saying. For example:*

"That's why the moon is so shiny. It's sparkling clean from all that licking. So there!

I bet you didn't know that."

Now add exclamation marks to the following passages from the book.

1. "You get a terrible stomachache. Then suddenly all the toast pops out of your belly button. So there "

2. "That's why the moon is so shiny.

   It's sparkling clean from all that licking.

   So there I bet you didn't know that."

(3) "Then the flowers go back into the ground
before anyone wakes up.

That's why they've got dew on them.

They're so sweaty from all that running around.
So there "

Make up your own sentences that need exclamation marks.

41

Glossary

stomp (-stomped) [v.] to walk with heavy steps, especially because you are angry

Smart Alec stomped into the room and said to them.

I bet to say that you are sure that something is true

I bet you don't know what the moon is made of.

lick [v.] to move your tongue across something

Lots of monkeys live on the moon and they lick the banana.

thread [n.] a long thin piece of a material such as cotton, nylon, etc.

Her little brother had tied a thread from her dress to the chair leg.

strut (-strutted) [v.] to walk in a proud way

Smart Alec strutted in and said.

stomachache [n.] a pain in your stomach

You get a terrible stomachache.

pop [v.] to come, appear, or move suddenly

Then suddenly all the toast pops out of your belly button.

belly button [n.] the small hollow in the middle of your stomach

Then suddenly all the toast pops out of your belly button.

head for (-headed) to move toward a place

Smart Alec picked up her lunch box and headed for the door.

Glossary

tangle (-tangled) `v.` to make a confused mass, especially of threads, hair, branches, etc.

It tangled itself around pieces of furniture.

weed `v.` to remove weeds from a piece of ground, etc.

Her friend Barney Gavarney was weeding the flower boxes.

race `n.` a competition between people, animals, cars, etc.

They play games and have races.

wake up (-woke) to stop being asleep

Then the flowers go back into the ground before anyone wakes up.

dew `n.` small drops of water that form on plants, leaves, etc. during the night

That's why they've got dew on them.

sweaty `adj.` wet with sweat

They're so sweaty from all that running around.

wind (-wound) `v.` to wrap something long around something else several times

She didn't know that the thread from her dress had wound its way through the school gate and round a tree.

march (-marched) `v.` to walk with regular steps

Smart Alec marched over to the dog.

Author: Danny Katz

Danny Katz writes for the *Age*, *Good Weekend*, and the *West Australian*. He is the author of the bestselling humor book, *Spit the Dummy*, and has also written several kids' books — not to mention, he says, a big-budget Broadway musical that nobody seems terribly interested in producing.

Illustrator: Mitch Vane

Mitch Vane has been working as a freelance illustrator for twenty years. Her work includes cartoons, book covers, advertising, and editorial illustrations, but most of her work is in children's book illustration. Her cartoons appear weekly in the *Age*.